ON THE QUEST

ON THE QUEST

A PATH LESS TRAVELED

JUSTIN ROSSETTI

To you, dear Seeker of Light & Life-

May this book be a lantern on your path,
a compass in the mist,
and a mirror reflecting the Divine spark within you.

May every page awaken who you truly are.
As you walk the winding way through realms of earth, fire, air,
and water, may you come to know that the quest is not to find
something lost, but to become all that was always within you.

And when you reach the mountaintop,
may you remember to look back with grace,
forward with faith, and inward with awe.

This journey is yours.
And you are ready.
Love, Truth, Peace, and Life

THE AWAKENING BEGINS
CONGRATULATIONS!

In your hand, you hold the answers to the questions you have been searching for. You no longer need to rely on another person to impart their wisdom. You don't need to attend another conference or follow a strict doctrine in your quest for spiritual attainment and purpose. The Kingdom of the Divine is, at last, within your grasp.

It is so close, in fact, that you will soon realize it has resided within you your entire life.

Many individuals long and thirst exhaustingly in their search for meaning and purpose. They look outward for answers, waiting for someone or something to deliver clarity. But only a vigilant few have found the secret formula for spiritual enlightenment—from within. I am here to share that secret with you.

You've likely always known there is more to life than what meets the eye. The emptiness and passion that relentlessly drove you in your search for fulfillment were not accidents. You were meant for this moment—right here, right now.

Only you know the times when you wanted to quit.

When fears, doubts, and insecurities overwhelmed you, you felt like giving up. But somewhere deep inside, a voice whispered to you. It reminded you that surrender was not an option. And it still isn't—because the Kingdom is at hand, and your time has finally come.

You are now open and ready to enter, receive your spiritual destiny, and begin seeing the world in living color.

This Is Your Awakening

You must awaken to the truth that you are perfect. No one's actions or opinions have ever made you less than what you truly are: divine royalty. It doesn't matter whether others love you, appreciate you, or approve of you. What matters is that you find the courage and self-confidence to know your identity—and to accept yourself completely.

It doesn't matter what past lives you've lived, what others have done to you, or what they failed to do. What matters now is that you stop complaining, stop blaming, and let go of the pain others have caused. True authority comes through your power to forgive, to heal, and to move beyond suffering.

When you stop judging and pointing fingers, you will begin to accept people as they are. And only then will you begin to accept yourself. Through that acceptance, peace and contentment will naturally be born—gifts that always emerge from forgiveness.

As you open yourself to new realms and different perspectives, you will begin to reassess and redefine who you are. This unfolding will reveal your truest self. And when you finally learn the difference between wanting and needing, you'll begin to release the doctrines and values you've outgrown—or those you should never have adopted to begin with.

You Are the Alchemist

You will learn that there is power and authority in your ability to create your own reality. You are your own alchemist. You shape your thoughts, and in doing so, you manifest them into consciousness. This is the sacred process through which your reality is born.

It is up to you to decide what happens next in this epic, self-actualizing journey.

So, join me now—on this quest to peel back the layers of outer influence and liberate your true self. It's time to grow. It's time to heal. It's time to embrace the love and success that have always been waiting for you.

Let's go!

A PATH LESS TRAVELED - PURIFICATION

LIGHTHOUSE – WHITE – CANDLELIGHT

You find yourself walking along a worn path through a thick forest. Every few seconds, bursts of color flash before you—first red, then orange, yellow, green, blue, and finally purple. Drawn forward by the rhythm of this mysterious light, you follow the path until it opens to a sandy bank beside a large, crystal-clear blue lagoon.

Across the lagoon stands a tall lighthouse, its spire reaching high into the sky. At its crown, a radiant lamp cycles through the same sequence of colors—red, orange, yellow, green, blue, and purple—casting beams across the water and horizon. At the base of the lighthouse is a small room with a crescent-arched wooden door.

Mesmerized, you turn your attention to the terrain but see no clear path around the lagoon in either direction. Studying the water, you estimate the distance to be less than five yards. The surface is calm, and when you dip your hand into it, you're surprised to find the temperature warm and inviting—safe enough, perhaps, to wade or swim across to explore the source of the lights calling to you.

You step into the water. The bank slopes gradually until

the water reaches your chest. It is peaceful, even buoyant, and soon you begin to float. Almost halfway across the lagoon, you swim forward, knowing you'll need to cross the last few yards by kicking or gliding. In a moment of trust, you submerge fully, letting the water envelop you from head to toe.

Suddenly, the water turns blood red and sweet as wine.

When you break the surface, your body is soaked in the red liquid. You can feel it saturating your skin, soaking into your pores and the very fibers of your being. Alarmed, you push toward the shore—the side nearest the lighthouse.

As you emerge, drenched and shaken, the lighthouse's light ceases rotating and fixes its beam directly on you. Vibrant colors flash through you like a spotlight on center stage. The rays pierce your skin and soul, burning away the blood red liquid with luminous energy. Startled but relieved, you scramble further up the sandy bank. As you safely reach the top of the sandy bank, the light cuts out. Darkness and silence return.

You sit, stunned and breathless, dazed by what just occurred. But after a long pause, courage wells up within you. With one deep breath, you rise—aware that something has changed. You begin to walk the path of the awakened.

The Guide of White Light

Standing on the bank, you now see a tall, radiant man clothed in white, surrounded by a glowing aura of brilliant white light. He appears between you and the lighthouse, majestic and beyond description. His presence moves you to your knees.

He steps toward you, gently placing a hand upon your

head. Instantly, the blood red and dampness vanish. Warmth fills your body, and you are dry.

A burst of white light flashes through you, pulsing from the crown of your head downward. Energy surges through your neck and shoulders, into your arms, torso, abdomen, and legs—wave after wave of radiant, pure white energy. It swirls around you in a mist that expands—first three feet, then six feet in every direction.

This light vibrates through every cell of your body, reaching deep into your mind and heart. You feel whole. Complete. Intimately connected to this being of light.

He begins to speak—not aloud, but telepathically. His words reverberate through every fiber of your being with profound resonance.

"The time is now. Be vigilant. There is much for you to learn. Consistent training is key to strength and growth. Use this time wisely to become strong. There are many challenges to overcome, and you must be prepared for every opportunity. Remember, we will be with you. You have the energy within you to succeed. Be of one mind, body, soul, and spirit. Remember, you can come back here anytime you need to recharge. We are with you always."

He helps you to your feet and embraces you with such compassion that your heart overflows. Tears stream down your face—not of sadness, but of joy and release. As he withdraws, he gently touches your cheeks, drying your tears.

Then he hands you a single burning candle placed in a brass candle holder.

Turning, he gestures to the lighthouse door behind him. As he disappears into light, you hear his final words:

"Go forth with courage. Be brave. We are with you."

Into the Tower

The wooden door of the lighthouse, is carved in a crescent arch, aged and weathered with a wrought iron ring on a chain for a handle. As your hand approaches it, the door swings open of its own accord. Darkness waits beyond.

You call out, "Hello?" Your voice falls flat. Silence answers.

You step inside, candle in hand. The small room at the base of the lighthouse reveals itself slowly by flickering light. The circular walls are built of large, stacked granite blocks—solid and ancient. There are no windows, no furnishings, no pictures—only the cold, dry air of stillness and stone.

As you step further in, you see to your right a black cast iron staircase spiraling upward along the curve of the wall. It rises in a counterclockwise motion, mysterious and foreboding. You move toward it—and suddenly, the door behind you slams shut.

Startled, you breathe deeply. In. Out. Calm returns.

In the dark, with only the warm flicker of candlelight, you remind yourself of how far you've come. You've crossed the threshold. Returning would mean swimming again. Forward seems the only option now.

With intention, you place one hand on the cold iron rail and carefully move your foot to the first step. You breathe again, steady and slow. One step. Then another.

The steps are made of the same granite as the walls, solid beneath your feet. You begin to ascend slowly, gripping the railing with one hand and holding the candle in the other. As your confidence grows, you climb a little faster.

Then doubt creeps in.

Was this the right path? Should you turn back? Was the

guide real—or a dream? You feel your heart beating faster. You don't know how high the stairs go or what you might encounter at the top. You're untrained, unprepared. But even as fear rises, a deeper pull urges you onward.

You complete one full rotation up the tower. Then a second.

As you near the second landing, you pause—uncertain. One more heavy step, and you find yourself at a small platform. A wooden door, embedded in the stone, awaits.

You place your hand on the wood. It opens with a soft creak.

Brilliant white light floods through the opening, blinding you momentarily after the long climb in darkness.

The Threshold of Choice

Now, standing at the door of radiance, you know this moment offers a choice. One voice whispers to turn back, descend the spiral, and retreat into what is known. Another beckons you forward into the unknown, where transformation awaits.

You've come this far. Something inside tells you that your best option—your *true* path—is to step through and discover what lies just beyond.

And so you do.

PART I

EARTH REALMS - TANGIBLE REALITIES

1

THE FIRST REALM: SPIRITS, GUARDIANS, & GUIDES

ELECTRIC BLUE – CRYSTAL WAND

You push against the door on the first landing inside the lighthouse until it opens wide and you step into the light of day. The warmth of the sun greets your skin—a sharp contrast to the cold stillness of the lighthouse. The brightness is nearly blinding, but your eyes gradually adjust. You find yourself standing at the edge of a small grove of trees, overlooking a lush, green meadow. Sunlight filters down in golden shafts through the leaves, and the air hums with vitality.

You step out from the trees, and the sight before you overwhelms your senses. A vast field of wild grass stretches out before you, speckled with vibrant flowers in full bloom. Their sweet fragrance washes over you like a wave. A pair of hares race past, playfully leaping through the grass. In the distance, you hear the faint sound of music—harps, flutes, and soft drums—and laughter echoing just beyond a gentle rise in the meadow.

Far beyond the meadow, a single majestic mountain rises into the sky, its gleaming white peak piercing the clouds. You pause to take in its grandeur, and then, drawn by the melody and joy, you begin walking through the grass toward the sound. With every step, you feel the energy of life coursing through your body—rising through your feet and ankles like a gentle electric current. It's like goosebumps—but better.

Birdsong fills the air in every direction. Out of the corner of your eye, you catch the blur of movement—just in time to see the largest buck you've ever witnessed leap into the woods.

As you near the top of the grassy knoll, the music becomes clearer. Harps sing, flutes flutter, and drums echo a pulse that feels in harmony with the life around you. When you reach the crest of the hill, the scene below takes your breath away.

The Gathering of Spirits

Radiant spirits dance and celebrate. Each one glows with its own distinct, vibrant hue. Though human in form—head, arms, torso, and legs—they lack distinct facial features or skin. They wear robes of light that match the hue of their aura: translucent shades of red, rose, magenta, lavender, plum, light blue, turquoise, teal, orange, yellow, gold, and every color in between. Some are four feet tall, others six, and a few appear round and jovial, like sprites or fairies.

You blink in disbelief.

The spirits seem to be having a joyful celebration. Some converse and laugh, others sing or play music. A few are seated in picnic fashion, while others dance freely. The energy of happiness is unmistakable. Your gaze locks onto a group dancing around a rainbow-colored maypole. Overcome with joy, you feel emotion rise within you. Suddenly, you burst into laughter—the most uninhibited, glorious laughter you've ever known.

This can't be real, you think. But does it matter? It feels *that* good.

Then—everything stops.

The music halts. The laughter fades. The spirits, mid-motion, all turn and look directly at you. Your laughter catches in your throat. Startled, you glance over your shoulder. Nothing is behind you. It's clear—they're all staring at *you*.

A surge of adrenaline hits, the ancient instinct of fight or flight awakening. And yet—you feel no danger.

In a flash of light, an authoritative figure emerges and stands before you.

The Electric Blue Guide

The spirit before you radiates a vibrant electric blue light. Tall and commanding, he appears male in stature, though his features remain ethereal. Like the others, he lacks skin but has attractive facial details. He is clothed in armor: a warrior's helmet, a breastplate, a sword sheathed at his belt, and a shield strapped across his back. Leather sandals wrap up to just below his knees. He is so tall that his knees meet your eye level—you must crane your neck to meet his face.

He greets you with outstretched arms and a warm smile.

Behind him, other spirits gather, curious but calm. Moved by awe, you bow low before the electric blue figure. In a gesture of mirrored respect, the spirits around him bow in return.

"Welcome," the electric blue being says, his voice deep and resonant. "We have been expecting your arrival. We are honored to receive you."

Then he adds, "I have a gift for you."

Before you can respond, he reaches into a leather pouch and draws out his closed fist. He extends it toward you and slowly opens his hand, revealing a small, crystal wand. He presents it to you with reverence.

Sensing your hesitation, he speaks again.

"The candle will only last so long," he says, "and you may wish to preserve it for another time and place. The crystal wand is our gift to you. You will come to rely upon it often for protection and strength."

You reach out to accept the wand. As you do, the guide says, "This gift will help illuminate your path. It will grant you access beyond. It is a tool for healing, for clearing, and for shielding you from negative energy."

Grateful, you raise the wand with both hands to share it with those gathered. The spirits cheer and applaud, their colors rippling with delight.

Then the electric blue guide's tone grows solemn.

"You must not linger. Go back the way you came— return to the place where your journey began and continue upward. Do not be tempted to descend back down the staircase. Your path is forward."

You nod, bolstered by his strength and reassurance. As you turn to leave, he calls out once more.

"There is one more thing," he says. "You may always return to this realm and spend more time here. However..." He pauses. "Before you do, focus on reaching the final ascension. As strange as it may sound, many who stop to smell the flowers become too distracted to finish the journey they came here to complete. So keep going. We will be here when you return."

You take in his words with care, bow once more in thanks, and make your way down the grassy knoll. The moment your feet touch the edge of the tree line, the door appears and swings wide open.

Before stepping through, you glance back for one last glimpse of the majestic mountain peak—still towering, now partially veiled by clouds that roll in from beyond the horizon. You breathe in deeply, letting purpose fill your lungs. Then you exhale, calm and steady.

With a clear heart and a steady mind, you walk through the door—this time not with uncertainty, but with confidence, excitement, and determination.

Because now, you *know*.

You're ready for what comes next.

2

THE SECOND REALM: NATURE

PEACH – CREEL BAG

After stepping back into the lighthouse and closing the door behind you, you pause for a long breath and release a deep sigh. The silence and darkness return once again. Is it relief you feel? Or disbelief? You're not quite sure how to interpret these unfolding experiences, but you allow the uncertainty to dissolve as your attention returns to the crystal wand in your hand.

The wand is smooth, round, and surprisingly small—yet its size doesn't diminish its significance. It feels like the most meaningful gift you've ever received. You stare into the clear crystal, entranced by how the remaining light from your candle reflects within it, sparkling like starlight. Only then do you realize how long you've been carrying the candle— its steady flame glowing warmly, though the weight in your arm now feels heavy.

You give the wand a gentle shake, then wave it through the air to see if something might happen. Nothing does. You shrug and smile to yourself, knowing it's time to continue upward. Holding the wand before you like a wizard for protection, you begin to ascend.

But something is different.

The staircase, which previously spiraled counterclockwise to the right, now ascends to the left in a clockwise direction. You pause, noting the shift. Though uncertain of its meaning, you know one thing for sure: you will not turn back.

You step forward.

One step. Then another. And another.

With each upward motion, the candlelight illuminates the narrow stairway. You feel more courageous—braver than you've ever felt before. After a full three-hundred-and-sixty-degree spiral, you lean toward the center of the spire, looking both up and down. But the light barely reveals more than a single rotation in either direction. Beyond that—only darkness.

You keep going.

Another rotation. Then another. Finally, you reach a small landing. As before, you expect a doorway—but this time, there isn't one. You glance around and spot a door set into the opposite side of the lighthouse wall, but there's no stairway or landing leading to it. It's completely inaccessible. Bizarre. You think to yourself, that *can't* be the right door, can it?

A choice presents itself: turn back or continue upward. But in truth, the choice is already made.

You move on.

As you ascend, your thoughts begin to wander. *Did I miss something? Was that strange, unreachable door important? Will there be another? What lies ahead? Will it get better—or worse?*

Fear, doubt, and anxiety begin to creep in like shadows. You keep walking, step by step, until another small landing appears. This time, there is a door—simple and within reach.

You extend your hand to the doorknob.

But there isn't one.

You push gently. Nothing. You push harder. Still nothing. Fortifying yourself, you raise the crystal wand and point it toward the door.

With a soft groan, the door slowly creaks open, releasing a cloud of thick, luminous steam that spills into the stairwell.

The Breath of Nature

You step forward, immediately swallowed by brightness and mist. The misty steam is dense—so thick you can't even see your own hand in front of your face. The crystal wand and candle offer no illumination here. Their light is drowned in the radiant fog. Still, the steam is warm, and though the air is heavy, it feels surprisingly gentle against your skin.

You wave your arms ahead of you to detect obstacles. With cautious steps, you move forward—ten, maybe twelve paces. You inhale deeply, and the moisture enters your nose and chest, coating your lungs like a think balm. It feels...relaxing as a sauna.

You close your eyes and breathe again. A second time. Then a third. Each breath fills you with tranquility. You feel your heart slow. Your muscles relax. A sense of peace envelops you.

When you open your eyes, the steam has cleared.

You find yourself at the edge of a crystal-clear lake. One more step and you would have tumbled into the water, where a single lotus bud floats gently on the surface. You lean down to observe it more closely and notice your candle has gone out—its flame extinguished by the mist. You set it aside and reach into the cool water to retrieve the lotus blossom.

Across the lake, about forty yards away, a waterfall spills from a rocky cliff, cascading down like liquid music. Its melody is soft and sweet—like the gentle notes of a piano. The sound washes over you like a healing touch. To the left and right, the lake stretches far, curving softly into the land.

You sit on the soft grass, captivated by the serenity of the scene. In the distance, you notice a silhouette—a bearded man in a wooden boat, slowly drifting across the water, enjoying a round piece of fruit.

Then, without warning, a peach-colored, radiant female figure appears beside you. She greets you warmly and sits down, her flowing dress matching the soft hue of her aura. She admires the lotus flower in your lap with quiet joy.

Setting a basket down beside her, she reaches inside and produces a plump, delicious-looking peach, offering it with a gentle smile.

Looking across the lake, she asks, "What do you see out there?"

You pause, searching for the right words.

Before you can respond, she says, "It's such a breath-taking place, isn't it?"

You reply by nodding in agreement, then hold out the lotus flower. "Would you like this? I found it here."

Her eyes widened. "Really? You would offer that to me? How delightful! Yes, please—what a precious and perfect gift. Thank you so much."

She continues, "For such a beautiful offering, allow me to return the favor." She holds out a small jute creel—delicately handwoven. "Tell me your material goals and desires. If I find any of them acceptable, I will approve one—or more—to come true."

You thank her, admiring the craftsmanship of the creel. It's just the right size to carry your candle, holder, and crystal wand. You laugh gently and admit, "Honestly, I'm not sure I even know what my material goals are. It feels like a big question—and I'd like to make sure I choose wisely."

With a playful tone you ask, "What are you, some kind of genie? Granting wishes you *approve* of? What counts as acceptable?"

The vibrant being laughs softly.

"I am the guardian of the four quarters," she says. "I see the four sides of human life as righteousness, true material needs and desires, abundance, and liberation. If I choose, I can approve what you ask for. That is the prerogative granted to me."

She leans in gently. "So, what would you like to make known? Will you choose wisely?"

You feel the answers stirring deep inside you. But you pause—taking a moment to reflect, to gather your thoughts, to weigh your heart. *There are so many possibilities... which ones should be spoken aloud?*

You inhale deeply. And with your next breath, you exhale the truth of your desires—clear, heartfelt, and unafraid.

The Blessing and Return

The radiant guide rises to her feet. She lifts her right hand and points toward the sky.

"May truth and peace be your guide," she says. "May your well-being be enhanced. Let the desires of your heart come true—and let what you receive be shared with others, to bring happiness to them as well as to yourself."

With that, her form begins to shimmer. The steam

returns—slowly thickening once again. You rise, securing the jute creel across your chest, your items now safely tucked inside.

You know it's time to go.

You make your way through the mist, moving swiftly toward the doorway before the fog becomes too thick to navigate. Just before your vision disappears completely, you spot the entrance.

You step back into the lighthouse.

The door closes softly behind you.

3

THE THIRD REALM: VISION
EMERALD GREEN – GEM

Having stepped back into the lighthouse spire and the door shut behind you, the familiar pitch-black silence envelops you once more. You reach into the jute creel, feeling around for your candle and crystal wand. Your fingers brush against something new—a small, hard object like a peach pit at the bottom of the bag. Curiosity flickers, but you return your attention to the task at hand.

You withdraw the crystal wand and, with a wave and a shake, you thrust it forward like a wizardly magician. A burst of light erupts from the round crystal tip, illuminating the darkness. Startled, you let out a shout of joy, jumping up and down in celebration. It works!

Exhilarated, you take a deep breath in and release it slowly. With the glowing wand in one hand, you begin to ascend the spiral staircase, now winding once again in a counterclockwise direction.

Your footsteps feel light. A bounce accompanies your stride as your thoughts drift to the previous guides—the gentle peach aura, the noble electric blue, and the luminous white. Each left their mark, and each realm brought you new understanding. As the memories stir, your mind begins to internalize the deeper meaning behind these encounters. The inward journey has begun.

The River of Reflection

Climbing steadily, your thoughts continue to turn inward. You begin to reflect on the risks you've taken and the rewards you've been given. You wonder about your role in these experiences—how much of this journey has been your doing? You think about your desires, your life purpose, your satisfaction—or lack thereof—with the current state of your life.

What do I really want?
What is my purpose?
Why am I here?

The questions swirl, unanswerable yet deeply familiar. They stir the dust of your inner world. Ideas about death, purpose, and the mystery of it all hover just beneath the surface. Surely there's a greater plan. There must be answers.

Lost in contemplation, you hardly notice you've climbed two full rotations. When you do, you find yourself standing on a new landing—at the foot of a third door.

You raise the illuminated wand. The door creaks open.

You pause at the threshold, inhale deeply, and exhale with purpose.

Then you step through.

The Realm of the River

The path ahead meanders gently to the left, bordered by knee-high grass swaying in the evening breeze. The light of day is slipping into twilight. To your right, a broad river flows—steady and swift, stretching over three hundred yards across. Far too wide and powerful to cross by swimming.

There is a shift in the air—subtle but distinct. This realm feels... different. Less comforting. The air smells crisp, like autumn. The path beneath your feet is more worn than those in previous realms, as though many others have passed this way before.

You walk alongside the river, your ears catching a faint clinking sound—metal on metal. You stop, listening carefully. The sound grows clearer. You detect the scent of smoke. Then—something else. Something foul.

Rot.

You cover your nose as flies begin to buzz around you in increasing numbers. A sense of unease creeps in. You crouch low in the grass, searching for cover as you forge ahead. Curiosity drives you forward, and you inch off the path, crawling slowly toward the source of the sound and smell.

You reach the edge of the tall grass and peer out.

The Dock of Despair

You've arrived at a river landing.

A dock juts out into the rushing water. You take shelter behind a stack of wooden crates. From here, you survey in silence.

A dark, shadowy spirit is working at a portable forge. He wears tattered black garments, and his presence radiates danger. The sight sends chills up your spine. Something in your bones knows—this is not a friendly being.

Beyond him, a caged wagon sits, holding ghostly, pearlescent human figures—bound in iron cuffs and chains. Two more dark spirits unload the souls one by one. You watch in stunned disbelief. Though the forms are ghostlike, they are still human—somehow decayed, rotting, surrounded by flies.

They are led to a table between two fire pits. A larger, commanding dark figure sits at the table, writing on a long scroll. He pauses to inspect each soul brought before him, then returns to his notes. Another spirit slams each soul into a small metal crate, locking the door behind them.

You glance behind yourself, realizing with horror that the crates you're hiding behind may also be holding souls. Your stomach turns.

You want to help. But how?

Scanning the area, your eyes catch movement. Two dark spirits escort seven frail humans down to the dock. They're loaded into a boat and pushed into the current. You watch helplessly as the boat drifts away.

Far in the distance, on the river, you spot a familiar sight—the old man from the last realm. He rows gently toward the drifting boat, though you can't quite make out what he's doing.

The Chains Within

Your heartbeat quickens.

Then you notice—the metal striking has stopped.

The dark spirit at the forge has walked away, leaving a hammer on the anvil.

Without thinking, you leap up, snatch the hammer, and race to the chained souls still standing in line. You prepare to break their bonds—only to discover something shocking.

There are no locks. The cuffs are closed, but unsecured.

You pull them apart. The chains fall.

You sprint to the crates and look inside.

One man sits huddled in the corner, arms wrapped around his knees. Another rocks back and forth, sucking his thumb. Another groans, his abdomen torn open. A fourth weeps quietly, what appears to be a gunshot wound leaking something unearthly from his skull.

None of them move. None seem to notice you. The crates have no latches, no locks. The doors can open—but none inside the crates have tried.

Desperation and sorrow surge through you. The pain is too much. The emotional weight crashes over you like a wave. You take a deep breath, trying to steady yourself. You *have* to help. You *must.*

You drop the hammer, swing open the nearest door, and reach for the cowering man inside. He recoils violently, scooting back as far as he can. He doesn't want to leave.

You touch him.

His pain becomes yours.

An ocean of sorrow floods into you. Your knees weaken. Your chest heaves. You scream—not in fear, but in raw empathy. Tears stream down your cheeks.

You stumble back, withdrawing your hand. You stand, overwhelmed, looking around for a way—*any* way—to help.

Out of the corner of your eye, you notice the movement of a dark spirits approaching.

"If you haven't figured it out by now, these people don't want help!"

The voice slices through the air. It belongs to a dark being—its tone mocking and sharp.

From every direction, dark spirits begin to converge on you, shadows of menace closing in.

Suddenly, a blinding emerald green light flashes, illuminating the dock with dazzling brilliance. A tall spirit guide, radiating the same emerald hue, appears between you and the approaching spirits. His presence is commanding, his eyes focused, unwavering. With swift resolve, he draws a sword from its sheath and steps into a defensive stance.

"Stay close," he instructs. "And whatever you do, don't get in those boats."

Two of the dark spirits draw their own blades and rush at him. In an instant, the emerald green being counters. He strikes the first, piercing it cleanly. A shriek erupts from the creature as it vaporizes into smoke and vanishes. The emerald green being turns with precision, slashing the second dark spirit with equal force—gone, just as fast.

With confident steps, the emerald green guide advances toward the table, where more dark spirits are gathering. Without hesitation, he lunges his sword toward the authoritative figure at the scroll. The being recoils, stepping back quickly into the fading twilight. Several of the lesser spirits rush to shield him, retreating with him until they disappear into the darkness.

You stand frozen in awe.

"Thank you," you whisper, your voice full of both reverence and relief.

The emerald green spirit guide sheathes his sword. "It is my pleasure," he replies calmly.

Breakers of Chains

"What is happening to these people?" you ask. "Why don't they want to be helped?"

The emerald green guide turns toward the caged souls, his expression both solemn and understanding.

"These are human souls," he says, "captivated by darkness and enslaved by demonic forces. They have lost hope—surrendered their sense of worth. Some chose this path consciously, others were led here unconsciously. Deceived by the traps of the enemy, they are bound to the lower realms. Most of them no longer believe they are worthy of freedom. It is heartbreaking... and it is becoming more common."

He pauses, his voice tightening.

"Hypocritical teachings, distorted doctrines, stifled spiritual growth, and endless worldly distractions—these are the poisons destroying many souls. They lose their way, forget their power, and settle for bondage instead of liberation."

"Is there any way to help them?" you ask. "There must be something we can do. We can't just leave them here... can we?"

The guide places a firm hand on your shoulder.

"Of course there's something we can do. And no, we won't leave them. In fact, you've already helped them simply by choosing to act. By showing up. By caring. Few do. But you—you are among the few."

You feel the weight of his words settle deep in your chest.

"Every soul has a choice," he continues. "To remain a slave to illusion, or to rise. To awaken. To remember the truth. Just as they chose, so can you—and so can those you're called to help. Freedom is always an option. But it starts within."

The Gift of the Gem

"I don't want to end up like them," you say quietly. "How do I protect myself from falling into that kind of despair? How do I help others avoid it? I want to set the captives free!"

The emerald green guide laughs warmly. "Ah, full of zeal —I knew it. That's why you're here. And yes, you *will* help others. But not before helping yourself. Your journey is still beginning. The path ahead is narrow, treacherous, filled with illusion. There is more to experience—more to learn."

He turns and points far into the distance. Beyond the hills, the last sliver of twilight illuminates a lone mountain peak.

"You must remain vigilant. That summit is your destination. There, all will be revealed. You cannot linger here. And whatever you do, do *not* step into a boat or onto the river. Not yet. This is not your time. Many lose their way by trying to skip the climb."

Then he gestures toward the riverbank, where a faint, lesser-worn path curves quietly beside the water.

"That is your road. Few find it. Fewer still succeed."

The guide steps closer, his eyes locking with yours. From a pouch at his side, he produces a small object and places it in your hand—a radiant precious gem, clear and bright as starlight.

"Take this for your protection," he says.

You turn it over in your hand, captivated by its glow.

"Thank you," you say. "But what is it for?"

"This gem will remind you of your purpose. You are the

breaker of chains—never forget that. Keep it close. One day, it will be far more valuable than the hammer you grabbed earlier."

He chuckles, and you smile faintly.

Creating Portals, Continuing Onward

"This gem," he continues, "is a key to higher realms. It will help you see through illusion. To use it, hold it between your thumb and second finger of your right hand. Point it outward and make a spiral motion. This will create a portal that reveals where you last left the path. You may use it to reenter where you left off, to continue, to rise."

You nod, holding the gem to your heart.

"From this point forward," he says, "you must *see* with inner vision. You must *feel* with your soul. You are moving into realms more spiritual than physical. Experience will be your compass."

You glance down at the gem. Then at the caged souls. Then back to the riverbank path winding forward into darkness.

You look up to salute the emerald green guide.

He returns your bow and vanishes.

You turn, and with one final glance behind, begin walking the narrow path less traveled.

Breath of Purpose

Some distance down the trail, you pause. The sounds of pain and sorrow still echo faintly behind you.

You close your eyes.

You take a deep breath in—and exhale, releasing the grief you absorbed from the souls you tried to save.

Another breath in—and out. This time, you feel a powerful connection to all living beings. A shared spirit. A shared struggle. A shared hope.

A third breath in. Slowly. Fully.

As you exhale, a calm peace settles deep in your chest.

You are ready for what comes next.

PART II

FIRE REALMS - TRANSFORMATION

4

THE FOURTH REALM: JUSTICE & RIGHTEOUSNESS

YELLOW – SCALES OF JUSTICE

When you open your eyes, the last rays of sunlight have vanished. Night has fully settled over the land. You glance skyward, but it's still too early for stars. Darkness surrounds you.

A flicker of panic rises in your chest.

Did I remember to close the lighthouse door?

Will the gem really work?

What if opening a portal was all fantasy—some mystical trick, or worse?

What if I'm trapped here forever?

You recall the electric blue guide's warning to keep moving forward, but the details blur. *What exactly did he say?* You struggle to remember. The memory dances just beyond reach.

You close your eyes and take a deep breath, slowly exhaling to center yourself.

You're here now. That's what matters. The narrow path ahead is still your best option. With courage stirring again, you remember the precious gem still in your hand. In your other, you retrieve the crystal wand from your creel. A confident wave brings its glow to life. The light shines onto the gem, revealing its brilliant facets.

That's when you recognize the gem, it's your birthstone.

You blink, startled. *How could the guide have known?*

Standing amidst the tall grass beneath the waxing crescent moon, you decide to follow the emerald green guide's instructions. You place the gem between your thumb and second finger and extend it outward, spiraling your hand in a circular motion.

Nothing happens.

You try again, this time adjusting your grip. Still nothing.

Feeling mildly ridiculous, you experiment with different hand positions and spiral motions, but no portal appears. With a shrug and a sigh, you tuck the gem into your creel. If there's no portal, there's still the path. You begin to walk.

The Castle in the Moonlight

The path becomes narrower as it leads into a grove of slender willow trees. Their long branches sweep downward like curtains, brushing your shoulders as you pass. The grove thickens with each step.

A half-remembered image from a childhood fairytale flutters into your mind. You can't recall the name of the story—but something about this place feels familiar.

Vibrant ferns rise from the forest floor. Flowers bloom with a soft, bioluminescent shimmer, casting silver hues beneath the moonlight. The path weaves away from the river, climbing through a series of steep switchbacks until it meets a road—a deeply grooved double rut, worn by time and travel.

To your left, the road disappears into the forest's depths. But to your right, silhouetted in moonlight, rises a castle.

Snow-capped peaks loom behind it—the same sacred mountain you've glimpsed before, shining high above the dark spires of the fortress.

You follow the rut road toward the castle.

Soon, you arrive at a moat and a wooden drawbridge. Beyond the bridge stands a tall gatehouse with double doors, flanked by burning urns, the entrance to the castle. No guards. No voices. Only the sounds of bullfrogs, crickets, and rustling leaves whisper on the wind.

You raise the crystal wand and aim it at the drawbridge. Only the gentle beam of light emerges.

You retrieve the precious gem again, holding it between your thumb and second finger. Pointing it toward the doors, you make a spiral motion. This moment is critical. If your visualization is strong enough, the drawbridge will lower. If not, nothing will happen.

You close your eyes, summon your will, and envision it clearly.

A creak. A groan. The chains begin to move.

The drawbridge lowers.

You walk slowly across, step by step. The gatehouse doors open before you. You pass into the gatehouse, and the doors close behind you with a thunderous echo.

The Corridor of the Mind

You emerge into a wide, marbled corridor. Warm light glows from sconces along the walls. The air is calm and still.

To your left and right, the corridor extends in both directions. You choose one and walk forward, marveling at the beauty and silence.

Doors of all shapes and sizes line both sides of the hall. Each one seems to call to a different part of you. Holding the gem in your hand, you open a door. Inside—nothing. You try another. Still empty.

Then, one door opens to reveal a room with carved symbols on the walls. They are unfamiliar, yet deeply personal. You feel as though the room knows you.

These are the mansions of your mind.

You continue opening doors, exploring room after room. Some are blank. Some filled with strange yet familiar etchings. Each space is sacred. Each one reflects something within you.

Eventually, the corridor loops back to your starting point.

But now, you notice a door you hadn't seen before.

You raise the gem, open the door, and step inside.

The Scales of Justice

You walk into a chamber lit by golden fire.

A yellow spiral flame bursts upward in the center of the room. From its core, a radiant female guide emerges—her form sculpted of living flame. She glows in vibrant shades of yellow, wrapped in golden energy.

In her hands, she holds a pair of scales.

They sway gently. Up and down. Back and forth.

She speaks, her voice soft yet commanding.

"Will you place the seed of your soul on the scale to discover whether you are worthy to begin the fertilization process?"

"Your seed will be weighed against fairness, harmony, and justice. The choice is yours—and yours alone."

You suddenly remember the small round peach seed

hidden at the bottom of your creel—the one given to you by the peach guide. Reaching down, you feel for it.

Your hand brushes the candle holder, the wand, the gem—and then something new.

A larger round object.

You pull it out.

A golden acorn.

It glows in your palm, radiant and warm, filling the room with brilliant golden light.

You reach into your creel and find the peach pit.

You step forward and gently place the acorn on one side of the scale and the peach pit on the other.

The scales tip.

Slowly rising and falling.

The scales move again, gently swaying.

And finally—balance.

The yellow guide smiles. "Congratulations. You are worthy."

She lifts the acorn with great care, enclosing it in her hand. Moments pass. When she opens her palm again, the acorn has transformed.

It is now a ball of flame.

The Flame Within

She steps toward you.

"You possess the elements within you. The reflection of yourself you have seen is righteousness."

She lifts the flaming acorn and gently presses it against your abdomen, just above your navel.

It sticks—without heat, without pain. You feel only tranquility.

Then she wraps the scales in a rich burgundy cloth, places them in a box, and hands it to you.

Finally, the fiery yellow guide vanishes—leaving you alone in the sacred silence.

But you are not empty.

You are ignited.

5

THE FIFTH REALM: SECRETS

ORANGE – COMPASS

S haking yourself out of a stunned daze, you place the box containing the scales of justice into your creel. You take a deep breath and exhale slowly. The chamber is quiet. You glance back toward the door you entered, but it is sealed tightly with no sign of a window or exit.

You know what must come next.

But will it work this time?

It has to.

A tingle of anticipation rushes through you. You reach into your bag and retrieve the precious gem. Holding it between your thumb and second finger, you begin making a spiraling motion in the air. Concentrating deeply, you focus all your energy and intention on creating an opening.

At first, nothing happens.

Then—something stirs.

A golden-yellow light begins swirling inside you where the acorn was placed, growing brighter with every inhale. With each exhale, it simmers and stabilizes. You take another deep breath. The energy surges and bursts outward, extending from your body like a spiral flare into the space before you.

All around you, a glowing spiral begins to take shape.

It's time to test your ability.

You visualize the circle expanding, widening into a portal. You imagine it becoming a tunnel—a hallway made of ancient stone and spiritual memory. When the image becomes clear, you take a leap of faith and step forward.

The Tunnel and the River

You descend into a dark, brick-lined passageway.

You slip the precious gem back into your creel, and you retrieve your crystal wand to light the way. The bricks are finely laid, clearly the work of master stonemasons. The corridor slopes downward gently but steadily. You move with caution, each step measured and mindful.

The light from your wand flickers across the walls, casting patterns that resemble dancing fairies. The hallway is remarkably clean—preserved as if by invisible caretakers.

Eventually, the tunnel opens into a vast underground chamber, where cobblestones line the banks of a flowing river. The water enters from a culvert to your left, curves sharply at the edge of a platform, and disappears into another tunnel to your right.

You pause, startled, as a boat approaches.

It's the old man again—the same one you saw on the lake, and later, on the river.

He signals you to get in.

You consider it. Say hello if you wish. Ask his name. Make conversation.

But remember the warning of the emerald green guide.

This man is a soul collector.

It is not yet your time.

When your conversation ends, you thank him and step away from the dock, continuing along the path beside the river. The tunnel narrows. Water drips from the ceiling above, and the dirt path beneath your feet turns to mud and puddles.

You walk for what feels like a long time, and then— distant light emerges.

Hammering echoes through the tunnel. The sound of metal striking metal grows louder with each step, reminding you of the dark spirits forge from the river dock.

Apprehension wells within you.

Still, you continue.

The tunnel opens into a workshop. It's small but warm and well-used. Tools hang from wooden beams, and black-smithing equipment is scattered throughout the space. In the center stands a forge, glowing with fire.

Bent over the furnace is a plump, orange-cloaked spirit guide, his back to you. His long beard matches the hue of his apron, and he wields a hammer with confident rhythm. Without turning around, he calls out with a cheerful voice.

"Hello! Come in, take a seat. I won't bite, I promise!"

You chuckle and sit down, noticing a wave of fatigue pass through you.

The Fires of Knowledge

The orange guide begins to speak. Stories of astrology, mythology, and ancient truths flow from him like an endless river. His energy is charismatic, almost theatrical. He doesn't skip a beat, his hands dancing in grand gestures to match his words.

As he talks, you feel a subtle vibration in the floor. You glance down, curious.

When the opportunity presents itself, you ask, "Why is the ground pulsing beneath me?"

Without missing a beat, he replies, "Ah! You're standing on the core of the Earth, the very heart of living consciousness. That rhythm beneath your feet? It's the heartbeat of the world."

He looks directly into your eyes, his expression flickering between wisdom and wild amusement.

"If you listen closely through the soles of your feet," he says, "you can connect with Mother Earth and gain knowledge about your own soul."

With that, he grabs a pair of tongs, lifts a glowing object from the forge, and quenches it in water. Steam hisses upward, carrying a fragrant scent that fills the air.

Turning to you with a spark in his eye, he asks, "Do you know the symbolic meaning of the compass rose?"

You begin to answer, but hesitate.

Not all who wander are lost, you think. *The compass always points north, so if you understand it, you're never truly lost.*

You consider saying something about the four directions. Sailors. Ships. Long journeys. You think of orientation, of spiritual guidance, of the stars.

Before you can speak, his voice enters your mind telepathically.

"Yes. That's all exactly right."

The Compass Rose

"The compass rose," he says aloud now, "is a symbol of spiritual awakening and discovery. Its four points represent infinite possibility, the past, the present, and the future. It's more than a tool—it's a guide, a teacher."

He walks toward you, his voice growing softer and more sincere.

"It always tells you which way is north—and north, throughout history, has symbolized progress and advancement. The compass, therefore, represents divine guidance. The North Star of the soul."

He continues, "The word 'compass' comes from the Latin *com*—meaning 'together'—and *passus*—meaning 'step or pace.' To compass means 'to step together.' To travel together. Using a compass signifies courage, independence, and the confidence to leave your comfort zone, knowing you will find your way."

He grins. "It even symbolizes luck. A lost traveler may find their path again, with just one glance at the needle."

He turns back to the forge, focusing intently.

Click.

"There we have it!" he exclaims. "Complete and in precise working order."

He turns and walks toward you with something in his hand.

A glowing, copper-alloy compass.

He holds it out with reverence.

You reach for it, taking the compass gently from his hand. Its beauty stuns you—an intricate design of gears, rings, and etchings, humming softly with energy.

"Thank you," you whisper, eyes wide with wonder.

Secrets and Departure

"Aww, shucks," he replies, blushing. "No need to thank me. I just hope it serves you well."

Then, with a warm and knowing tone, he adds:

"The secrets of the universe are love, truth, peace, and joy. Of these, love is the greatest. These are the hidden elements—the true keys to life everlasting."

He places his hand on your shoulder.

"Your journey must continue. Use the backdoor behind the forge to advance. And whatever you encounter next, do not fear. Have faith. Take courage. Follow the compass—and your heart."

You rise, thanking him for the gift and the wisdom. He nods, and you step quietly through the backdoor.

As it closes behind you, you feel a new strength rising within.

The compass rests in your palm.

And now you're more prepared than ever to take the next step.

6

THE SIXTH REALM: DEATH

SCARLET RED – SAGE & ASH

Beyond the workshop door, a flaming chariot awaits you. Four mares of different colors stand harnessed in front, their flanks gleaming in the flickering light. You step onto the chariot, letting your senses come alive as the horses pull ahead through the warm, rushing air. The team twists and turns sharply, then plunges down a steep slope that drops your stomach.

The descent ends, and the chariot levels out, pulling you through a pair of towering gates of flame. Inside the gated grounds, a procession of centurion spirits greets you. They stand like statues—each six feet apart—holding shields and spears with unwavering presence. The chariot rolls over a curved bridge above a steaming pool of thick, green bubbling water. You glance to the side and spot the old boatman again, calmly casting his fishing line into the bubbling muck from his boat.

Soon, you arrive at the outer edge of a vast garden nestled within the courtyard of a U-shaped villa. Long pavilion walkways extend left and right, lined with what appear to be stables or perhaps quarters. Towering trees stretch from the garden floor, their trunks rising beyond sight. Across the wooded garden, framed by these great trees, are the master living quarters. Your chariot comes to a stop at the garden's edge.

A scarlet red female spirit guide steps forward from the garden to greet you. She wears a flowing crimson gown, and her presence radiates strength and confidence.

"Welcome to the underworld," she says. "Please leave your ghosts of the past here before we begin."

Without another word, she turns and disappears into the garden. You hesitate, unsure what she meant—but you follow.

The Labyrinth of Roots

The path winds through the garden, twisting right, then left, enclosed by thick organic walls that resemble the interwoven roots of an ancient tree. Some roots appear healthy and strong, others dark, withered, or rotting. The walls rise high above, encircling you like the curvature of a great bowl. You realize now why the garden appeared raised from outside—it is the belly of a living labyrinth.

You follow the scarlet guide carefully, so you don't lose her. As the path continues, you begin to recognize the spiral form: a Chartres-style labyrinth, with many winding turns leading toward the center.

Eventually, you arrive at the center.

At the heart of the labyrinth lies a large brick ring, resting atop six petal-shaped brick steps. The scarlet red guide turns to you with solemnity.

"Please remove the masks of your personas," she says, "and toss them into the abyss."

If you already know what she means, you'll understand.

If not, ask her. She will help you identify the identities you've worn—those you've clung to and those you didn't know you carried.

Take your time.

With each mask you remove, feel the weight lessen. You may sense vulnerability rising within—but also, profound relief. One by one, you climb the petal steps and drop the masks into the circular abyss.

Red-hot flames rise to consume them. The fire crackles and roars. The guide captures several glowing embers in a small glass vial, corks it, and hands it to you. She smiles—a look of deep pride in her featureless face. For a moment, time ceases.

Then she speaks, not with her mouth, but directly to your soul.

The Fire of Transmutation

"Fire is spiritual energy," she says. "It can represent the lower nature—when ruled by impulse—or enlightenment when consciously awakened. Fire is the force of transmutation and regeneration. That is why you are here."

Her voice rings with clarity.

"I guided you through the garden so you could see the condition of your root system—how it connects to the tree of life. Some roots were strong, some exposed or decaying. With attention and nourishment, even the sickly roots will heal. Over time, you'll bear fruit—if you remain patient, grounded, and devoted to tending the soil of your soul."

She pauses, then continues.

"This realm exists between life and rebirth. It is a place to see what truly serves you—and what must be released.

There is no good or evil here, no moral judgment. Only recognition of what sustains you... and what doesn't."

You listen closely, still holding the glass vial of ashes.

"All too often," she says, "you grant access to the ghosts of the past. You drink the poison of resentment, fear, shame. It festers, infects, and weakens the roots. But you have the power to release it."

She steps closer.

"Now is the time to let go. Let fire do what it must. Through the flames you'll find healing. Fortitude. Liberation. But to step forward requires a sacrifice: Will you surrender yourself to the fire of the abyss?"

The guide extends her hand.

She is not pulling you—she is offering.

The Choice

A pause hangs in the air. She waits.

You feel the weight of the moment. If you're not ready to step into the fire, that's okay. There's no rush. You may choose to remain in the garden for now—to reflect, heal, and prepare.

This is the perfect time to practice **Ho'oponopono**, the ancient Hawaiian ritual of reconciliation and forgiveness.

Ho'oponopono means "to make right," to restore harmony and healing. It consists of four simple yet powerful statements, spoken either for yourself or on behalf of others:

1. *I am sorry.*
2. *Please forgive me.*
3. *I love you.*
4. *Thank you.*

You may say, for example:

"I am sorry for allowing fear into my life. I forgive myself for fearing the things I cannot control. I love who I am and who I'm becoming. I thank myself for growing and healing."

When you are ready—truly ready—accept the red guide's hand. She offers you a bundle of sage, then tosses more sage into the fire to stoke its sacred flames. Place the sage and vial of ash in your creel.

She nods.

You step forward.

Then, when you are ready—jump.

Rebirth in Flame

The fire rises to meet you—but it does not burn. The flames wrap around your body like a cloak, but the pain you expect never comes. The pit is shallower than you imagined—only knee to waist deep. Smoke and embers swirl, cleansing you. The impurities fall away. Your outer self begins to shimmer, becoming translucent. What remains is your true being— radiant, eternal.

You are being transformed.

And then—lifted.

Like a phoenix rising from ash, you begin to ascend. The fire becomes your wings. You soar higher, passing the roots of the garden, past the labyrinth's spiral path, above the steaming pool, and the chariot gates. From above, you see it all as if from another world.

You glimpse the scarlet guide below, still watching.

The underworld fades.

You drift higher, lighter, soothed.

Your eyes grow heavy.

And then—peaceful unconsciousness envelops you.

PART III

AIR REALMS - MYSTERIES OF FAITH

7

THE SEVENTH REALM: BEAUTY

PINK – ROSE OF SHARON OIL

You awaken gently from unconsciousness, lying flat on your back beneath a vast sky of swirling stardust. Spirals of light drift down in gentle cascades —some small and delicate, others grand and wide—each one glowing in hues of pink, violet, gold, and indigo. The moment feels dreamlike, yet more real than anything you've ever known.

Sitting up slowly, you feel the residual weight and wonder of your recent rebirth. The fire has changed you, transformed you, and now you rest in a realm of softness and serenity.

In the distance, a soft pink light flickers. It glows brighter as it approaches, revealing the form of a woman—a guide wrapped in a veil and modest gown, her presence radiant and maternal. As she nears, the falling spirals of stardust gather around her, settling softly on the ground like glimmering paint splatters.

The pink-colored guide uncorks a small alabaster jar and gently tips it over your head. A fragrant liquid pours out slowly, trickling down from your crown. You can feel it caressing your scalp, flowing down your temples, neck, and shoulders.

Without speaking, she bends down and lovingly takes your wrists. She turns your palms upward and pours a few drops into each hand. Then, placing a finger over the jar's opening, she flicks the liquid toward you, misting your body in a soft, fragrant shower.

You instinctively begin rubbing your hands together. The scent that arises is rich, soothing, floral—**Rose of Sharon**—and it wraps around you in a warm, embracing cloud. A feeling of peace and sacredness settles over you.

The rose pink guide anoints herself in the same way— oil on the head, in her hands, and across her veil. She sits across from you, cross-legged, and holds her palms out. A golden spiral of stardust falls gently into her hands, swirling and forming into a small oval shape. You both watch silently as the spiral condenses into a **seed**, shimmering and gold.

The seed begins to grow.

It stretches and expands, slowly transforming into the **form of a baby**, radiant and otherworldly. The guide draws the luminous infant to her chest and cradles it with reverence. She watches you with gentle eyes, and sensing your readiness, she leans forward, offering you the child.

You open your arms with care and awe.

The star baby is feather-light in your embrace. Its glow pulses with warmth, and its form continues to evolve as it grows in your arms. You feel a deep love rising within you— an instinct to nurture, protect, and adore this delicate being of starlight.

Around you, the falling stardust intensifies. The guide begins to speak—not with her voice, but through telepathic resonance. Her words ripple outward in waves of light, carrying messages of endearment, love, and welcome to the stardust that continues to descend. You realize she is speaking to all the emerging spirits in this realm.

You listen, and you understand.

Across the dark expanse, thousands—perhaps millions —of spirits are taking form. Some are only knee-high, others chest-tall. Each one shimmers in a unique color. They fumble and sway gently, still discovering their shape, their breath, their consciousness. Though they are not yet fully aware, you sense that their awakening is imminent. This is a place of birth, of beauty, of becoming.

You look down at the golden star baby in your lap, mesmerized by its gentle features, its glowing aura. You feel the vibration of its joy pulsing through your arms, into your heart, as it feeds off the affection you offer with every kind word you whisper.

"Can I keep it?" you ask softly, looking up at the rose pink guide.

She smiles with compassion.

"No," she replies gently. "It wasn't assigned to you."

You feel no disappointment—only reverence for the moment. You lean down and speak again to the glowing child, offering it words of love, encouragement, and blessings for the journey ahead. The infant glows even brighter in response. You feel its gratitude, wordless but pure.

The guide rises gracefully to her feet.

She takes the baby back into her arms, cradling it once more. Then, with a reverent bow, she turns and walks back in the direction from which she came. As she walks, the golden child nestled close, her form fades slowly—until she disappears entirely into the light.

You are left sitting in silence.

The Gift of Beauty

You may remain here as long as you wish. There is no rush in this sacred place. But when you are ready—when your heart is full—reach for the alabaster jar she left behind for you. Place it gently in your creel. Know that it contains more than oil. It holds blessing, grace, and the memory of love unspoken.

Take a deep breath in. Let it fill your chest. Then exhale, slowly, with gratitude.

You have just received a profound gift—one that marks a turning point in your spiritual journey. The seventh realm has welcomed you into the truth of beauty: the sacred power of life, love, and conscious creation.

When you are ready, rise and continue forward.

There is still more to discover.

8

THE EIGHTH REALM: REFLECTION

SILVER – MOONSTONE PENDANT

Using your precious gem, you create a portal in the same way you've done before. Darkness surrounds you momentarily—the familiar, endless void of space—until it transforms into a sparkling silver woodland. The trees glisten with reflected starlight. A bold full moon rises high above, its silver silhouette bright and commanding. All around, silver stars twinkle, and the entire forest glows with a mystical luminescence.

Tiny silver sprites emerge from the grass and foliage, unaware of your presence. They sing and dance joyfully, their voices light and chiming. A rushing river winds its way along the valley floor, reflecting moonlight as it flows. Electric silver currents pulse visibly through every living thing— racing through roots, flickering along tree trunks, dancing atop moonflowers. Everything is alive with energy, charged and humming.

You can feel that energy move through you too. It surges in waves from every direction, soaking into your skin, lifting your senses, expanding your mind.

And then you hear it.

A soft sobbing breaks the serenity. You turn toward the sound and discover a small girl, no older than six or eight, sitting on a log beneath the shimmering canopy. She wears a summer dress and glows with a soft pearlescent sheen. Her head is buried in her hands. She doesn't see you approach.

You kneel gently beside her.

"What's wrong?" you ask quietly. "Why are you crying?"

She lifts her head, startled. Pearlescent tears streak down her cheeks. For a few long moments, she says nothing.

Then, in a small voice, she replies:

"I'm lost. I don't know where I am."

You glance around the glowing silver forest. A sense of unfamiliarity lingers even in the beauty.

The girl begins to recount her story.

"My mom and dad were taking me to visit my Nana and Papa. On the way, I saw some kids playing near a tire swing hanging from a tall tree over a big hill. One boy swung out and jumped off—it looked like so much fun! I'd seen the swing before, but never any kids playing on it.

"When we pulled into Nana and Papa's driveway, I asked Mom and Dad if I could go swing with the kids. They said I could—after I said hello to Nana and Papa. So I jumped out, gave them both hugs and kisses, and ran toward the tree.

"There was a big truck parked near the road. Two men were working—one in the air inside a bucket, the other standing by the truck. I ran past them, and then I heard a loud *crack*. When I looked up, a huge branch was falling from the tree.

"The next thing I remember, I saw an ambulance. My mom and dad were getting inside. The lights were flashing, and it drove away fast. I don't understand why they left me there. I was just standing next to the branch.

"I ran toward Nana and Papa's house, but they were already leaving in their car. I waved and chased after them, but they didn't see me. So I ran back to the swing, but all the kids were gone. I sat by the tree waiting... but no one came. I must have fallen asleep. And when I woke up... I was *here*. In this black-and-white place I've never seen before."

You feel a pang in your chest.

"I'm so sorry for what's happened to you," you say gently. "But you're not alone anymore. I'm here to help you now."

The girl's eyes light up with a flicker of hope.

"Do you know the way?" she asks.

"The way?" you repeat, confused.

"Yes!" she beams. "We would love for you to show us the way."

Something in her words makes you pause.

"We?" you echo.

She smiles brightly and gestures around you.

From behind trees and bushes, dozens of **pearlescent silhouettes** emerge—men, women, children, even an elderly couple arm in arm. A mother holds a baby close to her chest. A young boy clutches a toy rabbit. Their eyes are soft and searching. They've been listening all along.

You turn, scanning the crowd, and then freeze. One of them... you recognize.

A familiar face stares back at you. It's a close relative—someone you hadn't thought about in years. He stands near the edge of the group, watching shyly as if uncertain he should step forward.

You call out to him and rush to meet him.

"Do you know me?" you ask.

He smiles warmly. "Yes... I know you. It's so good to see a familiar face. But why are you here? What happened? Why aren't you... like the rest of us?"

You reassure him that nothing has happened to you, that as far as you know, you're still alive and well.

"How long have you been here?" you ask.

His expression turns somber.

"Since the day I passed, I suppose. You remember that time, don't you? We heard this is the place where lost souls come—the ones who never found the keys of enlightenment. We're waiting... hoping someone will show us the way to everlasting life.

"We've been here a long time. More arrive every day. But no one has found the path out. It's... it's a dismal place. Not painful, exactly—but empty. Colorless. We exist, but we don't grow. We just wait."

He looks at you with pleading eyes. "What year is it? How long has it been?"

You don't answer immediately. Your mind races. Time feels distorted here. Whatever this realm is—*whatever it means*—you know now that your journey is far more than personal.

You are here to illuminate the path for others.

Bridge Between Realms

Lost in a sudden epiphany, you turn to the crowd and call out, urging them to follow you. You gently grasp the young girl's hand and signal for the woman holding the infant to stay close. With your ancestor at your side, you begin walking, intentionally ignoring his question about the year and how long he has been in this place. You remind yourself that the answer is irrelevant now—perhaps even better left unknown.

You retrace your steps along the path you took earlier, trusting your instincts. With each step, the trail of pearlescent human silhouettes behind you grows longer, winding across the woodland. You scan your surroundings for familiar markers. Spotting the glowing, reflective river, you feel a surge of hope. Surely the river leads to the source—that's why no one is meant to enter it or take a boat. Being swept downstream would mean passage to the source, but no return to this reality.

Reaching the riverbank, you search the flowing silver water. You look upstream and down, hoping to see the old man in his boat, but the river is empty. You press forward upriver, trying not to reveal your rising anxiety. You walk for what feels like hours, the procession behind you trudging faithfully along. Then, at last, you catch a glimmer in the distance.

There—casting a wide net into the middle of the river—is the old man.

You wave frantically, calling out to him. The old man hauls in his net, heavy with glistening fish, and slowly drifts toward the shore. When he reaches you, he greets you with a knowing smile.

"Are you ready to take a ride in the boat?" he asks.

Relieved, you respond, still uncertain how to explain this moment to the others. You ask if a few can ride with him.

"I have room for three," he replies. "Let the fish be given as a gesture of goodwill to those on the shore."

You help unload the heavy net, handing it off to the gathered souls. Then, without delay, you lift the little girl into the boat.

"What are you doing?" she asks, uncertain.

"Don't be afraid," you whisper. "Trust that you are going to arrive exactly where you're meant to be."

You reach your hand out to the woman with the infant. She passes you the child, and once she's safely aboard, you return the baby to her arms. Then you signal your familiar ancestor.

He shakes his head, hesitant. "No. There are too many others. I can't go before them."

You rest a hand on his shoulder. "It's your time now. Go with them. Help look after the child. Watch over the woman. They will need you."

He gazes at you, eyes welling with tears, then nods and climbs in. You give the boat a gentle push, sending it off into the glowing, reflective river.

As soon as the boat drifts from the shore, a sudden blast of trumpet sound rings from further up the riverbank. You spin around.

A brilliant, blinding silver light approaches. The other pearlescent silhouettes scatter in all directions, terrified by the source of the sound. The trumpet rings out again—this time the sound is a rushing wave of force that pushes against your chest like a powerful gust of wind. A third blast sounds, almost knocking you backward.

From the center of the radiance, a tall silver male spirit steps forward. He wears a long tunic with a hood resting behind his head, and in his hands, he carries the radiant trumpet.

"You have done well," he says. "Your desire to set souls free is noble and worthy of honor."

You bow your head and humbly thank him. "Will the ones in the boat be alright?" you ask.

"They are safe," the silver guide answers. "They are headed on, in the right direction."

You glance at the forest and back at him. "Why did the others run when you arrived?"

He looks around, then turns to you with a calm expression. "What others?"

You hesitate. "The ones behind me... the crowd..."

He nods thoughtfully and begins walking up a soft path curving deeper into the forest. You follow as he speaks again.

"It is admirable to help those you can. But know this—you cannot save everyone. The work of liberation is sacred, but it is not without limits. These souls have made their choices and are bound to their consequences. Free will is a profound gift, but it also carries responsibility. Everlasting life comes through sacrifice, and not all are willing to walk that narrow road."

He stops and turns toward you.

"But *you* are willing. You have demonstrated compassion, empathy, initiative, and humility. That is why you have come this far."

He reaches into the folds of his tunic and presents a radiant silver stone pendant hanging from a fine chain.

"This is a gift," he says. "A moonstone, symbolic of new beginnings. It is yours in honor of your selfless act. It will protect you—against harm, against accident, against energetic loss. Unlike other gifts, you need not learn to wield it. You will simply notice its presence: an illumination of mind, an enhancement of intuition, clarity in divine connection. Do you accept it?"

You feel the weight of the moment and nod. "Yes. I accept."

The silver guide steps forward and gently places the cord of the pendant around your neck. As the moonstone rests against your chest, waves of energy pulse outward. You feel it ripple through you—your feet, your hands, your crown. Your vision flickers. Everything becomes blurry and electric.

The guide snaps his fingers several times, bringing you back into focus. You blink rapidly, anchoring yourself.

"Now," he says, pointing to a doorway hidden behind silvery vines, "continue your path."

You thank him with all your heart, bowing deeply in gratitude. Then, without hesitation, you step forward, part the vines, and pass through the doorway into what awaits.

9

THE NINTH REALM: ILLUMINATION
VIOLET – CRYSTAL ORB

Stepping through the doorway, you find yourself once again enveloped in familiar darkness. You reach into your bag, draw out the crystal wand, and activate it with a confident wave. A soft glow radiates outward, revealing your location within the lighthouse spire.

A sense of unease ripples through you. There's no door at this level to close behind you. A troubling thought crosses your mind—if any of the white-silhouetted souls discovered this threshold, could they follow you through? You're inclined to wait and find out, but feel a sense of urgency in continuing. Pressing forward, you assess your elevation within the lighthouse by leaning over the railing, peering into the blackness below.

You know what must be done. You begin the climb upward.

One full spiral rotation. Then a second. A third. A fourth. At four and a half, you pause to peer out a deeply set cathedral window. Climbing onto the ledge, you gaze out. The lagoon shimmers far below in the moonlight, and beyond that, across the sprawling forest, a curtain of fog meets the trees like a vast, silver sea.

You estimate you're at least a hundred feet above the ground. Drawing in a deep breath, you reflect on how far you've come—and how much farther you may have to go.

You resume the ascent, counting each full spiral as you go: five... six... seven... eight...

At the ninth full spiral, you reach a landing—but there is no door. This is unusual. Every previous landing featured a doorway. You glance upward. The faint light from above seems just as far away as when you began.

Rather than continue upward, you retrieve your precious gem and create a portal as you've done before. You extend your arm, spiraling outward toward the smooth lighthouse wall. Light spirals begin to form. A portal opens wide enough for you to pass through.

On the other side, you are greeted by a stunning sight: a sleigh waits on a wide runway. Harnessed to the sleigh are four great winged beasts, each with a distinct form—one appears as a man, another as a lion, one as an ox, and the last as an eagle. Perched at the sleigh's front is a pure white dove, serene and still.

You move closer, marveling at the craftsmanship of the sleigh and the presence of these majestic beings. As you do, a dazzling violet guide appears before you. She is radiant, feminine in stature, with expansive violet wings and a flowing violet gown.

She smiles. "Would you like to take a ride with me?"

You nod, unsure whether you're more excited or awestruck. You climb into the sleigh, settling into the plush bench seat. The violet guide joins you, taking her place beside you.

With a signal of the reins, the winged beasts begin to

gallop forward. The sleigh surges ahead, picking up speed along the runway, and then—liftoff.

As the sleigh rises into the air, the runway fades beneath you. Ahead, the sky is alive with the vibrant colors of morning. The first rays of the rising sun stretch across the horizon, illuminating your path. You soar higher, and the snowy mountain peak now seems within reach—though the slopes remain steep and formidable.

Leaning over the edge, you spot the enchanted woodland. The river you followed earlier winds alongside it. You trace its path back to the castle—the very one you entered in the Fourth Realm. From this vantage, you can see a large courtyard in the heart of the castle, its centerpiece a single mighty oak with wide-spreading branches. The castle's full structure becomes clear: the inner bailey, the keep, the high battlements, and the thick ramparts encircling everything. The drawbridge is now raised, the moat surrounding the walls.

Your gaze continues, following the river, seeking familiar landmarks. You hope to locate the landing where you once encountered the lost souls and dark spirits—but from this height, you begin to question your sense of direction.

"This is a glimpse of where you've been," says the violet guide, her voice soft but clear. "And a glimpse of where you are going. Look carefully. Beyond the castle, there is only one path that ascends the mountain. That is your destination."

You squint to see the path she speaks of—it is indeed narrow and winds steeply upward toward the snowy peak.

She continues, "If you thought the path until now was difficult, the journey ahead is even more demanding. The climb will require everything you've learned—every gift you've been given. Fortitude. Strength. Faith. Keep your eye on the summit. We are all cheering for your success."

She reaches under the sleigh seat and retrieves a glowing object. Cradled in her hand is a crystal orb, gleaming with inner light.

"With this orb," she says, "you will gain greater intuition and deeper connection to the Divine. It will reveal truth—about yourself and the world. It will also allow you to receive direct communication from the Divine: wisdom, warnings, guidance. And you may speak back through it, as well. Would you like to try?"

You accept the orb, holding it in your hands. As your gaze sinks into its depths, you feel a stirring in the center of your forehead. Your third eye opening.

At first, it's a tingling sensation—like tiny sparks across the skin. Then it becomes a pulsing, rhythmic pressure. A vision emerges: roots, pure and unblemished, growing at miraculous speeds. There is no rot, no decay. They expand, growing stronger, yet remain exposed and vulnerable. You feel their sensitivity. These roots absorb energy—colors, vibrations, light—rapidly and fully.

The violet guide nods. "Ah, yes. In choosing forgiveness and compassion, deep healing has taken place. Painful memories are transforming into strength. What you see is the beginning of enduring spiritual growth—a return to divine origin and purpose. This is the threshold of righteous perfection."

Suddenly, you feel the sleigh begin to descend.

The wind rushes past, loud in your ears, the sensation exhilarating. The descent grows steeper, then gentler, guiding the sleigh to a graceful landing atop the castle rampart above the gatehouse.

The violet guide rises and steps down from the sleigh,

motioning for you to do the same. You carefully place the crystal orb into your creel, then follow her lead, stepping onto stone.

Your knees buckle slightly under the weight of the moment. You pause, steadying yourself.

The violet guide offers no farewell. She simply bows, returns to the sleigh, and departs into the sky—leaving you alone, standing atop the stronghold of all you've journeyed through.

PART IV

WATER REALMS - ROYAL AUTHORITY

10

THE TENTH REALM: STRENGTH
GOLD – SIGNET RING

S tanding on the castle rampart, you glance down and notice several feathers scattered at your feet— remnants left behind by the winged beasts of the flying sleigh. You kneel, pick one up, and inspect it for a moment before gently placing it into your bag. The weight of your satchel is growing, filled with the many gifts and tools gathered along your journey.

You pause to watch the sunrise on the eastern horizon, the warm glow stretching across the sky. Then you turn and peer over the opposite side of the rampart, looking down into the castle bailey you glimpsed from above during your flight. Beyond the bailey, across the courtyard and behind the keep in the heart of the castle, lies your next destination.

Following the rampart walkway, you make your way to the nearest battlement entrance and descend a flight of wooden steps, reentering the castle's interior halls. You feel a quiet thrill at the chance to revisit this sacred place, but a gentle voice within reminds you not to linger too long. You will have the opportunity to return whenever you wish.

As you pass through the familiar corridors, the rooms appear changed—transformed. One chamber is filled with shimmering gold: bars, coins, goblets, swords, and ornate armor. Another is lavish with books, another with silk linens, blankets, and luxurious pillows. You sense these treasures are not locked away—they are available to you, to take and use freely as needed. Another room overflows with spices, herbs, and exotic teas, alongside tools for crafting potions, brews, or restorative blends. You pause to take in the scents, colors, and sensations, appreciating the abundance.

When ready, you continue your journey around the connected halls—completing one full circuit, then another, and a third. At last, you arrive again at the door where you once met the fiery yellow guide. You enter, closing the door softly behind you.

You walk directly forward, toward the far wall of the chamber. As you approach, you notice something remarkable—the wall appears to have a glass like sheen. Upon closer inspection, you realize it's not a wall at all, but a smooth, cascading waterfall flowing from a narrow crevice near the ceiling. You lean in. Your reflection shimmers across the surface. Reaching out, you touch the water. It does not feel wet. You push your hand deeper and feel—nothing. There's no barrier behind.

With faith in your heart, you take a step forward and pass through the slick cascading water.

You emerge onto a red carpet that gently slopes downward toward a grand dais at the far end of a vast, domed chamber. You pause, taking in your surroundings. The space resembles a majestic amphitheater or sacred auditorium. On either side of the central aisle stand rows of ornate wooden desks, each paired with a plush chair, all facing a dais at the other end of the vast room. The space feels regal —holy.

Tall marble walls rise up from the chamber floor, their surfaces adorned with intricate carvings and towering stained-glass windows. Vivid light filters through, painting the lower chamber in brilliant hues. High above the marble walls, balcony seating climbs so steeply that the uppermost rows vanish into shadow. Two elevated balconies flank the dais—one to the upper left, one to the upper right—clearly designed for the attendees of honor. In the center of the dais stands a great throne, flanked by several regal chairs on either side.

As you slowly walk down the red carpet, your eyes are drawn to the grandeur and solemnity of the throne. The chamber is silent, but alive with anticipation.

From behind the left side of the dais, a figure enters. He moves with purpose, his presence unmistakable. The guide is cloaked in gold.

"Greetings to you," he says warmly.

"Hello," you reply. "What is this place?"

"This is the throne room of the Divine," the golden guide explains. "The dais before you holds the sacred throne of the Most High. The two upper balconies are for the seraphim and cherubim. The tiered seating encircling the chamber is for those who lived pure of heart and made great personal sacrifices so others might live eternal. The desks below are for the elders—those who have been granted wisdom and authority. Every soul will eventually walk this red carpet, standing before the glory of the Divine."

"Why is the room empty now?" you ask.

"The chamber is not currently in session," the guide answers. "But come—would you like to sit on the throne?"

You hesitate, then nod. Together, you ascend the steps to the right of the dais. The golden guide steps aside, allowing you to approach the throne. With a nod of reassurance, he signals that it is safe to sit.

You lower yourself into the seat. It feels powerful—royal. From this position, you can imagine the chamber full of celebration, praise, and divine ceremony. You envision all eyes turned toward the throne, bathed in light and glory.

"Would you like to know where your seat is?" the guide asks.

You look up. He gestures to a specific area in the stadium seating.

"There," he says. "That's your place. And it's a good one —an honored one. You should feel proud."

Pride and humility rise together in your heart. It is a tremendous honor—but also a solemn responsibility.

"Just wait until you see who you'll be seated next to," he adds with a knowing smile. "I'll leave that as a surprise. You'll be delighted, I'm sure. But for now, your path continues. Before you go, I have a gift."

He produces a gleaming gold signet ring.

"As you may know," he says, "the signet ring was a symbol of authority. It sealed royal decrees, ratified laws, and marked proclamations. This ring grants you similar power—the power to enact, declare, and transform. It is the authority of the righteous leader, and it is now yours."

You slip the signet ring onto the little finger of your non-dominant hand. It flares with golden light before settling into a soft, steady glow.

The guide turns and leads you behind the dais, down

the opposite stairs. At the rear, he pulls aside a heavy, veiled curtain.

"Peace be with you," the golden guide says.

You nod your thanks, heart full, and step forward through the curtain—into the next phase of your sacred journey.

11

THE ELEVENTH REALM: MERCY & GRACE

TURQUOISE – COAT OF MANY COLORS

You emerge from the majestic throne room into a space that is unfamiliar and charged with expectancy. A cool, crisp mid-morning breeze brushes across your face like a gentle welcome from the Divine. You blink in the natural light. Above you is an extended awning, dark in hue, arching out from the wall like the wing of some cosmic structure, shielding you from the gentle rain that falls in rhythmic drops. Directly in front of you is a heavy black curtain that conceals your view, and to your left, a wide opening reveals a partial glimpse of what lies ahead.

You hear it before you see it—lively, resonant shamanic drums pounding with ceremonial precision, followed by the deep harmonic cadence of chanting voices. There's something primal yet elevated about it, as if the sound is not just music, but invocation—an ancestral memory rising into the present moment. You are no longer in a place of private reflection; you sense that what lies beyond the curtain is a space of gathering, of revelation, of celebration.

Taking a few tentative steps forward, you realize where

you are. You're just off-stage in a celestial amphitheater; a sacred arena opens to the sky. You pause, feeling the gentle rain touch your skin—more mist than droplets—yet somehow each contact is charged, purposeful, like a blessing rather than a nuisance. You peer out toward the stage, and what you see takes your breath away.

Before you, an audience of infinite depth—souls in silhouette, their outlines human yet glowing with vibrant, marbled hues. Not white, not gold, not silver—but every conceivable color, mixed and refracted like the surface of an opal. As the soft rain falls upon them, each drop triggers a transformation. New colors emerge in response, radiant and living, as though the rain activates something dormant within. You feel a wave of awe as you watch the living sea of rainbow spirits rejoice, dance, and sing. It is so vivid, so beautiful, that you briefly wonder whether you are hallucinating. Yet your heart tells you this is more real than anything you've experienced before.

From the opposite side of the stage, a figure steps into view and the curtains open in dramatic fashion. The guide is masculine in form, cloaked in a radiant turquoise garment that seems stitched from light and water. His movements are fluid, his presence luminous. He strides with purpose to the center of the stage, where a large, polished turquoise altar rises like an island amid celebration. When the crowd sees him, a wave of joyful applause erupts. Some spirits clap. Others raise their hands. Some twirl in celebration. The colors ripple like auroras.

The music dims. The drums keep their heartbeat rhythm, steady and grounding. The turquoise guide raises his arms, and silence falls with reverence. Then, without speaking aloud, his voice fills the amphitheater—not through sound, but telepathically, in a collective field of knowing. You hear his words not with your ears, but with your heart.

"At this hour, we are gathered together in celebration as one family.

United as brothers and sisters, I invite you to bear witness to this sacred moment.

Today, we honor the triumph over trials, the transformation of suffering into wisdom,

The sacred victories of love over fear, truth over illusion, peace over chaos, and joy over despair.

These are the keys that open the gates of everlasting life."

The guide turns to face you and gestures for you to come forward.

You step onto the stage. The rain continues to fall, soaking into your skin with electric intimacy. It's more than water—it's energy. You feel it activating every cell in your body, stirring something primal and eternal within. As you approach the turquoise altar, the audience shifts in unison to face you. The weight of a thousand unseen eyes settles on you, not as pressure, but as blessing. You stand tall, eyes forward, heart open.

The closer you stand to the altar, the more intense the energy becomes. The raindrops now land like tiny sparks of divine current. Each one sends tingles through your scalp, down your spine, into your fingertips and toes. The sensation grows—not painful, but overwhelming in its immensity. You have to ground yourself with conscious breath just to remain upright, to not fall to your knees in reverence. You are fully seen. Fully known. Fully received.

Then, a sudden crack of thunder splits the sky. A lightning bolt arcs down, not with destruction, but with glory. It strikes among the crowd, not harming, but electrifying.

Their cheers erupt again, louder, more passionate, more alive. The drumming intensifies. The chants rise like a tide. Beyond them, looming in mist and majesty, the mountain—the final ascent—rises into view. You know, with every fiber of your being, that you are near the culmination of your path.

Suddenly, from the front rows of the crowd, a hand waves frantically. Your gaze is drawn to the familiar face of the little girl you helped onto the boat, beaming with delight. Beside her stands the man you also helped—his eyes wet with emotion, a proud smile spread across his face. Seeing them here, vibrant and free, confirms everything. You did help them. They made it. Your actions mattered. The moment overwhelms you. Tears spring unbidden, and you let them fall—tears of joy, of relief, of sacred knowing.

The turquoise guide raises his hand again, and the crowd quiets. The drumming softens, the chanting fades to a hum. The turquoise guide gestures for you to step up onto the altar. You obey, climbing the few steps and turning to face the souls below.

The guide begins a chant—mysterious and ancient. You do not understand the words, but you feel their power resonating through your bones. Then he speaks again, addressing the entire gathering.

"To be robed in the Garment of Divine Color is to wear the mark of transformation.

Not all who pass through life are prepared to carry such light.

For this robe is not given to the untried or the proud.

It is reserved for those who have surrendered, suffered, sacrificed, and been reborn.

It is woven from mercy and dyed in grace.

To wear this is to walk in the authority of the Divine."

He lifts a garment—radiant, flowing, multicolored. It is like Joseph's coat of many colors, but more vivid, more celestial. Each patch shimmers with its own hue and memory. He gently places your left arm through one sleeve, then your right, then settles the garment over your shoulders like a mantle of heaven itself.

"Now," he says, "by the powers vested in me,

I complete this coronation."

A roar of celebration erupts. Music explodes. The drums shake the ground. Voices rise. The amphitheater becomes a living cathedral of color and sound. You feel the power surging through you. The garment amplifies it, conducts it, makes it visible. Your very skin glows with sacred fire.

The turquoise guide takes your hand and calls your name. He leads you slowly off the stage. Down a hidden stairwell, away from the cheers and color, the sound becomes muffled behind you. The door ahead opens. Another threshold appears.

Your journey continues—but you now walk robed in divine mercy and wrapped in eternal grace.

12

THE TWELFTH REALM: CLARITY

INDIGO – BROOCH

At last, after all your journeying through realm after realm, you arrive at the heart of the castle—the sacred courtyard. A stillness surrounds the space, deep and ancient, as though even time itself bows in reverence here. Towering at the center, rooted in majesty, stands a mighty oak tree. Its broad trunk radiates with power, and from its roots pulses an energy that feels unmistakably alive. Thick tendrils of bark reach through the stone courtyard like veins through skin, merging the organic with the constructed, the eternal with the temporal.

You pause, letting your eyes travel upward through the vibrant green canopy that arches above you in a dome of life. From this ground-level perspective, the oak is not only larger than it first appeared from above, but infinitely more profound—like a being that has always been with you, silently guiding your path, now revealed in its fullness. It is more than a tree. It is a memory. A mirror. A home.

Just beyond its massive roots, nestled slightly to the side, is a circular pool of crystalline water. In its center rises an elaborate fountain sculpted with artistry beyond earthly imagination.

Jets of water surge upward with gentle strength before cascading down, flowing into layered troughs. From there, four distinct streams spill outward in perfect symmetry—north, south, east, and west—cutting across the courtyard like rivers of destiny. The soft, musical rhythm of the water creates a sacred soundscape that seems to harmonize with your very heartbeat.

You approach in silent awe. Dancing between the droplets, water nymphs materialize—luminous, laughing, childlike spirits. They leap and play with unburdened joy, scattering light across the stone like scattered diamonds. It is a realm untouched by sorrow. A place beyond time.

Hidden just behind the oak tree is a stone bench, half-shielded from view by a gentle cascade of low-hanging branches. It calls to you with a quiet invitation. With no one else present in this tranquil sanctuary—at least nonvisible—you accept the offer. You settle onto the bench and inhale deeply, letting the breath fill your chest. Then, slowly, you exhale. Again. And again. Each breath sinks you deeper into stillness, until even your thoughts seem to evaporate in the peace of the moment.

Without realizing it, you drift into a meditative state. It is not sleep, but it is also not awaking. It is a state of sacred openness. And it is there, in that space between worlds, that a being of indigo light appears beside you.

The guide is silent at first, seated comfortably, their presence exuding wisdom and calm. Then, with a voice that seems to emerge from both within and beyond, the messenger speaks:

"This place is most holy and sacred. It is the inner sanctum of the soul.

It represents the Source—the origin of all movement, all being, all love.

These waters were the first breath of life, and this oak, their child, is the tree of your soul.

You once received a seed—the divine spark—and planted it deep within your spirit.

And over time, through storm and sunlight, through joy and anguish, you nurtured it.

You chose to heal. You chose to grow. You chose to remember who you are."

The indigo guide turns to face you fully, their expression gentle and sincere.

"You already know this truth. You feel it now. This courtyard is not somewhere *out there*—it lies within.

It is your origin and your return.

This tree is the full flowering of your spiritual maturity. This water, the memory of your immortality.

This moment—this breath—is the revelation of your Soul."

You feel a warmth rise in your chest. It is not the fire of transformation nor the rain of cleansing, but something else. A serenity. A wholeness. It is the feeling of arrival.

The guide continues, voice now tinged with reflection:

"Not many make it this far. So many seekers get lost early in the lower realms, pacified by distraction.

Some awaken only to burn out in the fire realms—too frightened of what purification might reveal.

Others rise into the air realms but get lost in abstraction, fear, or the endless opinions of others.

But you... you have stayed the course.

You held fast to love, to truth, to peace, to joy.

You cultivated inner authority. You remembered your divine inheritance.

And now you are here—at the spring of life itself."

The fountain bubbles beside you as the guide gestures toward it.

"The fountain is the soul of humanity. The water, its spirit.

Every soul is fed from this Source, and every soul may return to it.

When you feel dry, come here and drink.

When you feel weary, come here and rejuvenate.

When the world feels heavy or hostile, return to this water and drink.

It will always be waiting. It flows not just for you, but through you."

The messenger pauses and then adds, with a knowing smile:

"And remember—I am the Messenger. I carry your requests to the Divine, and I return the answers.

Every petition, every longing, every cry of your heart—delivered.

Be sincere. Be intentional. I do not alter the message. I only carry it."

There is a pause. The water nymphs quiet. The tree seems to lean in as if listening.

Then the guide stands and reaches into a pouch at their side, retrieving a radiant indigo brooch.

"I now entrust you with this brooch.

It is a symbol of sacred authority and enlightenment.

It is the key to every threshold in the lighthouse, and a beacon to all who still wander.

Wear it openly. Wear it wisely.

It marks you not as one who knows all, but as one who *remembers*—and who *guides* others to remember too."

You accept the brooch and pin it near your heart.

Instantly, a subtle heat radiates from it—not burning, but vibrant, alive. You feel it merging with your essence.

The messenger places a hand on your shoulder and speaks the final words:

"Your Soul is immortal. The only death is that of illusion.

The only loss is forgetting.

You have died to the world and been reborn into eternal life.

Now, for the final act... take the plunge.

Step into the fountain. Do not fear.

You will not drown. Now it is time to live eternally."

You rise, drawn not by command but by destiny. Slowly, reverently, you approach the center of the pool. You step into the water. It is cool but not cold, welcoming but powerful. With one final breath, eyes closed, heart wide open—you surrender plunging into the Fountain of Eternal Life.

PART V

THE FINAL ASCENT

13

DIVINE GLORY

RAINBOW

A long, distant trumpet blast stirs you from unconsciousness.

Your eyes flutter open to find yourself lying on a soft, sandy riverbank. The roar of rushing water can be heard nearby. You sit up slowly, dazed but intact, and glance around, orienting yourself. The river is flowing faster than you've ever seen it move—its current powerful and wild. Only a few yards away, the sound of trumpet blasts grows deafening. You rise to your feet, following the sound until you arrive at the edge of a towering cliff. There, you're met with a breathtaking sight: a massive fifty-foot waterfall cascading with unrelenting force.

You exhale in quiet gratitude that you had washed ashore just in time. Just a bit further and you would have gone over the edge.

Looking upstream, your eyes trace the source of the water. High in the castle wall, a stone culvert pours forth water into the moat, which then spills dramatically out toward the cliff's edge. The sunlight glints off the falling water, refracting a vibrant rainbow. The cascading water becomes a luminous bridge of light, a living arc of color and promise.

Following the path of the rainbow with your eyes, you now realize you are outside the castle once again, but not as you were. Your soul has been reshaped and remade.

In the distance at the end of the rainbow, your gaze lands upon a golden gate nestled into the base of a mountainside. Beyond the gate, golden stairs rise with steady grandeur, climbing the mountain in perfect alignment with the end of each color of the rainbow. And once again, the trumpet sounds—this time from the very top of the mountain, a call echoing across heaven and earth.

You approach the gate and pass through without resistance. The golden stairs welcome you with quiet nobility. With each step upward, you feel your body responding—not just physically, but spiritually. Green hills roll beside you for a time, lush with vegetation, before gradually giving way to a thick mist. The fog embraces you like a cloud of mystery and transition.

The trumpets sound again. Louder. Closer. You press forward, your vision limited but your heart full. Emerging on the other side of the fog, the landscape has changed. The lush earth has become dry, dusty, and sun-drenched. Still, the golden stairs remain, gleaming against the arid terrain like the thread of destiny pulling you ever higher.

A third blast of the trumpet rings out, long and commanding. It fills your lungs with fire and resolve. Your legs burn, but you ascend. Right foot, left foot. Step after golden step. The air thins. The path steepens. But you continue.

Snow appears in patches, then ice. A cold wind lashes your face. Still, you hold fast, ascending with unwavering faith. You feel the sun above you, radiant and strong, beckoning you onward. The peak is just beyond reach—so close now that your soul surges with hope.

And then, you arrive.

With one final step, you crest the summit.

The trumpets explode in glorious harmony, no longer a blast but a full symphony, announcing your arrival with majestic fanfare.

Before you is a vision beyond imagining—a realm of indescribable beauty. A world crafted not from stone and mortar, but from light, color, sound, and love. A paradise of perfect balance, where every realm you've passed through now merges into one harmonious whole.

Fields of radiant flowers ripple in the wind. Birds of luminous feathers soar overhead. Pools of crystal water sparkle like diamonds beneath a golden sun. Water nymphs splash joyfully between lotus blossoms. Sprites dance hand in hand through luminosity. Even the clouds themselves seem to shimmer with sentience.

This is it—the convergence of all that was, is, and ever shall be.

Along the edges of this sacred place stands an army of spirits—rainbow-cloaked, vibrant, and alive. They wait in solemn formation, shining with reverence. As you walk through this oasis, twelve familiar figures come into view. Six stand on your left, six on your right—the twelve guides who journeyed with you through each realm. Each guide is now fully radiant, standing in ceremonial reverence.

The trumpets shift into a melody—bold, grand, yet tender. The air hums with sacred energy. Rainbow spirals of glittering light swirl gently from above, falling like blessings around you. You feel them on your skin—tingling, transformative, transcendent.

A voice calls out, resonant and loving.

"We have all waited a long time for you to arrive. Welcome home. We are so proud of you."

Your gaze moves past the two lines of guides. At the end of the path, robed in glory and radiant beyond comprehension, stands the embodiment of the Divine.

"I am so delighted to reveal Myself to you," the Divine says.

"I hope you enjoy this place, and I hope the gifts I prepared for you have been useful—beautiful reminders of who you are.

My child, I offer you one more gift before you go. My blessing. Come closer and receive it."

With your heart wide open, you walk between the rows of guides. As you pass, each one bows, honoring your journey. You ascend the final steps and stand before the Divine.

The Divine reaches out and places a hand gently upon your head.

"You have learned all the lessons," the Divine whispers.

"You have died in order to live.

You have surrendered, in order to receive.

Your Soul is immortal. I love you."

The Divine wraps you in an embrace—deeper, warmer, and more complete than any embrace you've ever known. It is love beyond form. It is healing beyond words. It is home.

Then the Divine leans close, whispering into your ear:

"There is still more for you to do on Earth.

Your journey there is not yet complete.

You carry a purpose, and there is a plan.

The spirits and guides will remain with you—to help, to bear witness, and to guide others.

This is only the beginning... of an everlasting relationship."

As the Divine's voice trails off, the twelve guides begin to sing.

Their song is celestial—a harmonic chorus of light and love. The vibration is so high, so beautiful, that your physical senses begin to blur. You feel yourself slipping—not downward, not inward-back toward the place from which you came, yet will never the same.

The song continues as you gently fade into unconsciousness and awaken in consciousness.

As reality sets in, somewhere deep inside, you know the truth:

You have been to the mountaintop.

You have tasted eternity.

You carry the Divine within you.

And the journey... has only just begun.

MAY YOU REMEMBER

The labyrinth was never meant to confuse,
but to consecrate.

The ascent was never meant to be easy,
but to make you whole.

And the Kingdom of the Divine has always resided
within you.

May you find yourself, fully and fearlessly, and in so doing,
become a beacon of light and life for others still wandering.

Love, Truth, Peace, and life